The Fugitive

MAVEN BOOKS

The Fugitive

Rabindranath Tagore

MAVEN BOOKS

Chennai Trichy New Delhi

MAVEN BOOKS

An Imprint of **MJP Publishers**

ISBN 978-93-87488-09-0 **Maven Books**

No. 44, Nallathambi Street,
Triplicane, Chennai 600 005

MJP 388

Publisher : **C. Janarthanan**

Publisher's Note

The legacy of a country is in its varied cultural heritage, historical literature, developments in the field of economy and science. The top nations in the world are competing in the field of science, economy and literature. This vast legacy has to be conserved and documented so that it can be bestowed to the future generation. The knowledge of this legacy is slowly getting perished in the present generation due to lack of documentation.

Keeping this in mind, the concern with retrospective acquiring of rare books has been accented recently by the burgeoning reprint industry. Maven Books is gratified to retrieve the rare collections with a view to bring back those books that were landmarks in their time.

In this effort, a series of rare books would be republished under the banner, "Maven Books". The books in the reprint series have been carefully selected for their contemporary usefulness as well as their historical importance within the intellectual. We reconstruct the book with slight enhancements made for better presentation, without affecting the contents of the original edition.

Most of the works selected for republishing covers a huge range of subjects, from history to anthropology. We believe this reprint edition will be a service to the numerous researchers and practitioners active in this fascinating field. We allow readers to experience the wonder of peering into a scholarly work of the highest order and seminal significance.

Maven Books

Contents

1

Darkly you sweep on, Eternal Fugitive, round whose bodiless rush stagnant space frets into eddying bubbles of light.

Is your heart lost to the Lover calling you across his immeasurable loneliness?

Is the aching urgency of your haste the sole reason why your tangled tresses break into stormy riot and pearls of fire roll along your path as from a broken necklace?

Your fleeting steps kiss the dust of this world into sweetness, sweeping aside all waste; the storm centred with your dancing limbs shakes the sacred shower of death over life and freshens her growth.

Should you in sudden weariness stop for a moment, the world would rumble into a heap, an encumbrance, barring its own progress, and even the least speck of dust would pierce the sky throughout its infinity with an unbearable pressure.

My thoughts are quickened by this rhythm of unseen feet round which the anklets of light are shaken.

They echo in the pulse of my heart, and through my blood surges the psalm of the ancient sea.

I hear the thundering flood tumbling my life from world to world and form to form, scattering my being in an endless spray of gifts, in sorrowings and songs.

The tide runs high, the wind blows, the boat dances like thine own desire, my heart!

Leave the hoard on the shore and sail over the unfathomed dark towards limitless light.

2

We came hither together, friend, and now at the cross-roads I stop to bid you farewell.

Your path is wide and straight before you, but my call comes up by ways from the unknown.

I shall follow wind and cloud; I shall follow the stars to where day breaks behind the hills; I shall follow lovers who, as they walk, twine their days into a wreath on a single thread of song, "I love."

3

It was growing dark when I asked her, "What strange land have I come to?"

She only lowered her eyes, and the water gurgled in the throat of her jar, as she walked away.

The trees hang vaguely over the bank, and the land appears as though it already belonged to the past.

The water is dumb, the bamboos are darkly still, a wristlet tinkles against the water-jar from down the lane.

Row no more, but fasten the boat to this tree,—for I love the look of this land.

The evening star goes down behind the temple dome, and the pallor of the marble landing haunts the dark water.

Belated wayfarers sigh; for light from hidden windows is splintered into the darkness by intervening wayside trees and bushes. Still that wristlet tinkles against the water-jar, and retreating steps rustle from down the lane littered with leaves.

The night deepens, the palace towers loom spectre-like, and the town hums wearily.

Row no more, but fasten the boat to a tree.

Let me seek rest in this strange land, dimly lying under the stars, where darkness tingles with the tinkle of a wristlet knocking against a water-jar.

4

O that I were stored with a secret, like unshed rain in summer clouds—a secret, folded up in silence, that I could wander away with.

O that I had some one to whisper to, where slow waters lap under trees that doze in the sun.

The hush this evening seems to expect a footfall, and you ask me for the cause of my tears.

I cannot give a reason why I weep, for that is a secret still withheld from me.

5

For once be careless, timid traveller, and utterly lose your way; wide-awake though you are, be like broad daylight enticed by and netted in mist.

Do not shun the garden of Lost Hearts waiting at the end of the wrong road, where the grass is strewn with wrecked red flowers, and disconsolate water heaves in the troubled sea.

Long have you watched over the store gathered by weary years. Let it be stripped, with nothing remaining but the desolate triumph of losing all.

6

Two little bare feet flit over the ground, and seem to embody that metaphor, "Flowers are the footprints of summer."

They lightly impress on the dust the chronicle of their adventure, to be erased by a passing breeze.

Come, stray into my heart, you tender little feet, and leave the everlasting print of songs on my dreamland path.

7

I am like the night to you, little flower.

I can only give you peace and a wakeful silence hidden in the dark.

When in the morning you open your eyes, I shall leave you to a world a-hum with bees, and songful with birds.

My last gift to you will be a tear dropped into the depth of your youth; it will make your smile all the sweeter, and bemist your outlook on the pitiless mirth of day.

8

Do not stand before my window with those hungry eyes and beg for my secret. It is but a tiny stone of glistening pain streaked with blood-red by passion.

What gifts have you brought in both hands to fling before me in the dust?

I fear, if I accept, to create a debt that can never be paid even by the loss of all I have.

Do not stand before my window with your youth and flowers to shame my destitute life.

9

If I were living in the royal town of Ujjain, when Kalidas was the king's poet, I should know some Malwa girl and fill my thoughts with the music of her name. She would glance at me through the slanting shadow of her eyelids, and allow her veil to catch in the jasmine as an excuse for lingering near me.

This very thing happened in some past whose track is lost under time's dead leaves.

The scholars fight to-day about dates that play hide-and-seek.

I do not break my heart dreaming over flown and vanished ages: but alas and alas again, that those Malwa girls have followed them!

To what heaven, I wonder, have they carried in their flower-baskets those days that tingled to the lyrics of the king's poet?

This morning, separation from those whom I was born too late to meet weighs on and saddens my heart.

Yet April carries the same flowers with which they decked their hair, and the same south breeze fluttered their veils as whispers over modern roses.

And, to tell the truth, joys are not lacking to this spring, though Kalidas sing no more; and I know, if he can watch me from the Poets' Paradise, he has reasons to be envious.

10

Be not concerned about her heart, my heart: leave it in the dark.

What if her beauty be of the figure and her smile merely of the face? Let me take without question the simple meaning of her glances and be happy.

I care not if it be a web of delusion that her arms wind about me, for the web itself is rich and rare, and the deceit can be smiled at and forgotten.

Be not concerned about her heart, my heart: be content if the music is true, though the words are not to be believed; enjoy the grace that dances like a lily on the rippling, deceiving surface, whatever may lie beneath.

11

Neither mother nor daughter are you, nor bride, Urvashi.[1] Woman you are, to ravish the soul of Paradise.

When weary-footed evening comes down to the folds whither the cattle have returned, you never trim the house lamps nor walk to the bridal bed with a tremulous heart and a wavering smile on your lips, glad that the dark hours are so secret.

Like the dawn you are without veil, Urvashi, and without shame.

Who can imagine that aching overflow of splendour which created you!

You rose from the churned ocean on the first day of the first spring, with the cup of life in your right hand and poison in your left. The monster sea, lulled like an enchanted snake, laid down its thousand hoods at your feet.

Your unblemished radiance rose from the foam, white and naked as a jasmine.

Were you ever small, timid or in bud, Urvashi, O Youth everlasting?

Did you sleep, cradled in the deep blue night where the strange light of gems plays over coral, shells and moving creatures of dreamlike form, till day revealed your awful fulness of bloom?

---

1. The dancing girl of Paradise who rose from the sea.

Adored are you of all men in all ages, Urvashi, O endless wonder!

The world throbs with youthful pain at the glance of your eyes, the ascetic lays the fruit of his austerities at your feet, the songs of poets hum and swarm round the perfume of your presence. Your feet, as in careless joy they flit on, wound even the heart of the hollow wind with the tinkle of golden bells.

When you dance before the gods, flinging orbits of novel rhythm into space, Urvashi, the earth shivers, leaf and grass, and autumn fields heave and sway; the sea surges into a frenzy of rhyming waves; the stars drop into the sky—beads from the chain that leaps till it breaks on your breast; and the blood dances in men's hearts with sudden turmoil.

You are the first break on the crest of heaven's slumber, Urvashi, you thrill the air with unrest. The world bathes your limbs in her tears; with colour of her heart's blood are your feet red; lightly you poise on the wave-tossed lotus of desire, Urvashi; you play forever in that limitless mind wherein labours God's tumultuous dream.

12

You, like a rivulet swift and sinuous, laugh and dance, and your steps sing as you trip along.

I, like a bank rugged and steep, stand speechless and stock-still and darkly gaze at you.

I, like a big, foolish storm, of a sudden come rushing on and try to rend my being and scatter it parcelled in a whirl of passion.

You, like the lightning's flash slender and keen, pierce the heart of the turbulent darkness, to disappear in a vivid streak of laughter.

13

You desired my love and yet you did not love me.

Therefore my life clings to you like a chain of which clank and grip grow harsher the more you struggle to be free.

My despair has become your deadly companion, clutching at the faintest of your favours, trying to drag you away into the cavern of tears.

You have shattered my freedom, and with its wreck built your own prison.

14

I am glad you will not wait for me with that lingering pity in your look.

It is only the spell of the night and my farewell words, startled at their own tune of despair, which bring these tears to my eyes. But day will dawn, my eyes will dry and my heart; and there will be no time for weeping.

Who says it is hard to forget?

The mercy of death works at life's core, bringing it respite from its own foolish persistence.

The stormy sea is lulled at last in its rocking cradle; the forest fire falls to sleep on its bed of ashes.

You and I shall part, and the cleavage will be hidden under living grass and flowers that laugh in the sun.

15

Of all days you have chosen this one to visit my garden.

But the storm passed over my roses last night and the grass is strewn with torn leaves.

I do not know what has brought you, now that the hedges are laid low and rills run in the walks; the prodigal wealth of spring is scattered and the scent and song of yesterday are wrecked.

Yet stay a while; let me find some remnant flowers, though I doubt if your skirt can be filled.

The time will be short, for the clouds thicken and here comes the rain again!

16

I forgot myself for a moment, and I came.

But raise your eyes, and let me know if there still linger some shadow of other days, like a pale cloud on the horizon that has been robbed of its rain.

For a moment bear with me if I forget myself.

The roses are still in bud; they do not yet know how we neglect to gather flowers this summer.

The morning star has the same palpitating hush; the early light is enmeshed in the branches that overbrow your window, as in those other days.

That times are changed I forget for a little, and have come.

I forget if you ever shamed me by looking away when I bared my heart.

I only remember the words that stranded on the tremor of your lips; I remember in your dark eyes sweeping shadows of passion, like the wings of a home-seeking bird in the dusk.

I forget that you do not remember, and I come.

17

The rain fell fast. The river rushed and hissed. It licked up and swallowed the island, while I waited alone on the lessening bank with my sheaves of corn in a heap.

From the shadows of the opposite shore the boat crosses with a woman at the helm.

I cry to her, "Come to my island coiled round with hungry water, and take away my year's harvest."

She comes, and takes all that I have to the last grain; I ask her to take me.

But she says, "No"—the boat is laden with my gift and no room is left for me.

18

The evening beckons, and I would fain follow the travellers who sailed in the last ferry of the ebb-tide to cross the dark.

Some were for home, some for the farther shore, yet all have ventured to sail.

But I sit alone at the landing, having left my home and missed the boat: summer is gone and my winter harvest is lost.

I wait for that love which gathers failures to sow them in tears on the dark, that they may bear fruit when day rises anew.

19

On this side of the water there is no landing; the girls do not come here to fetch water; the land along its edge is shaggy with stunted shrubs; a noisy flock of *saliks* dig their nests in the steep bank under whose frown the fisher-boats find no shelter.

You sit there on the unfrequented grass, and the morning wears on. Tell me what you do on this bank so dry that it is agape with cracks?

She looks in my face and says, “Nothing, nothing whatsoever.”

On this side of the river the bank is deserted, and no cattle come to water. Only some stray goats from the village browse the scanty grass all day, and the solitary water-hawk watches from an uprooted *peepal*aslant over the mud.

You sit there alone in the miserly shade of a *shimool*, and the morning wears on.

Tell me, for whom do you wait?

She looks in my face and says, "No one, no one at all!"

20

KACHA AND DEVAYANI

Young Kacha came from Paradise to learn the secret of immortality from a Sage who taught the Titans, and whose daughter Devayani fell in love with him.

Kacha: The time has come for me to take leave, Devayani; I have long sat at your father's feet, but to-day he completed his teaching. Graciously allow me to go back to the land of the Gods whence I came.

Devayani You have, as you desired, won that rare knowledge coveted by the Gods;—but think, do you aspire after nothing further?

Kacha: Nothing.

Devayani: Nothing at all! Dive into the bottom of your heart; does no timid wish lurk there, fearful lest it be blighted?

Kacha: For me the sun of fulfilment has risen, and the stars have faded in its light. I have mastered the knowledge which gives life.

Devayani: Then you must be the one happy being in creation. Alas! now for the first time I feel what torture these days spent in an alien land have been to you, though we offered you our best.

Kacha: Not so much bitterness! Smile, and give me leave to go.

Devayani: Smile! But, my friend, this is not your native Paradise. Smiles are not so cheap in this world, where thirst, like a worm in the flower, gnaws at the heart's core; where baffled desire hovers round the desired, and memory never ceases to sigh foolishly after vanished joy.

Kacha: Devayani, tell me how I have offended?

Devayani: Is it so easy for you to leave this forest, which through long years has lavished on you shade and song? Do you not feel how the wind wails through these glimmering shadows, and dry leaves whirl in the air, like ghosts of lost hope;—while you alone, who part from us, have a smile on your lips?

Kacha: This forest has been a second mother to me, for here I have been born again. My love for it shall never dwindle.

Devayani: When you had driven the cattle to graze on the lawn, yonder banyan tree spread a hospitable shade for your tired limbs against the mid-day heat.

Kacha: I bow to thee, Lord of the Forest! Remember me, when under thy shade other students chant their lessons to an accompaniment of bees humming and leaves rustling.

Devayani: And do not forget our Venumati, whose swift water is one stream of singing love.

Kacha: I shall ever remember her, the dear companion of my exile, who, like a busy village girl, smiles on her errand of ceaseless service and croons a simple song.

Devayani: But, friend, let me also remind you that you had another companion whose thoughts were vainly busy to make you forget an exile's cares.

Kacha: The memory of her has become a part of my life.

Devayani: I recall the day when, little more than a boy, you first arrived. You stood there, near the hedge of the garden, a smile in your eyes.

Kacha: And I saw you gathering flowers—clad in white, like the dawn bathed in radiance. And I said, "Make me proud by allowing me to help you!"

Devayani: I asked in surprise who you were, and you meekly answered that you were the son of Vrihaspati, a divine sage at the court of the God Indra, and desired to learn from my father that secret spell which can revive the dead.

Kacha: I feared lest the Master, the teacher of the Titans, those rivals of the Gods, should refuse to accept me for a disciple.

Devayani: But he could not refuse me when I pleaded your cause, so greatly he loves his daughter.

Kacha: Thrice had the jealous Titans slain me, and thrice you prevailed on your father to bring me back to life; therefore my gratitude can never die.

Devayani: Gratitude! Forget all—I shall not grieve. Do you only remember benefits? Let them perish! If after the day's lessons, in the evening solitude, some strange tremor of joy shook your heart, remember that—but not gratitude. If, as some one passed, a snatch of song got tangled among your texts or the swing of a robe fluttered your studies with delight, remember that when at leisure in your Paradise. What, benefits only!—and neither beauty nor love nor…?

Kacha: Some things are beyond the power of words.

Devayani: Yes, yes, I know. My love has sounded your heart's deepest, and makes me bold to speak in defiance of your reserve. Never leave me! remain here! fame gives no happiness. Friend, you cannot now escape, for your secret is mine!

Kacha: No, no, Devayani.

Devayani: How "No"? Do not lie to me! Love's insight is divine. Day after day, in raising your head, in a glance, in the motion of your hands, your love spoke as the sea speaks through its waves. On a sudden my voice would send your heart quivering through your limbs—have I never witnessed it? I know you, and therefore you are my captive for ever. The very king of your Gods shall not sever this bond.

Kacha: Was it for this, Devayani, that I toiled, away from home and kindred, all these years?

Devayani: Why not? Is only knowledge precious? Is love cheap? Lay hold on this moment. Have the courage to own that a woman's heart is worth all as much penance as men undergo for the sake of power, knowledge, or reputation.

Kacha: I gave my solemn promise to the Gods that I would bring them this lore of deathless life.

Devayani: But is it true you had eyes for nothing save your books? That you never broke off your studies to pay me homage with flowers, never lay in wait for a chance, of an evening, to help me water my flower-beds? What made you sit by me on the grass and sing songs you brought hither from the assembly of the stars, while darkness stooped over the river bank as love droops over its own sad silence? Were these parts of a cruel conspiracy plotted in your Paradise? Was all for the sake of access to my father's heart?—and after success, were you, departing, to throw some cheap gratitude, like small coins, to the deluded door-keeper?

Kacha: What profit were there, proud woman, in knowing the truth? If I did wrong to serve you with a passionate devotion cherished in secret, I have had ample punishment. This is no time to question whether my love be true or not; my life's work awaits me. Though my heart must henceforth enclose a red flame vainly striving to devour emptiness, still I must go back to that Paradise which will nevermore be Paradise to me. I owe the Gods a new divinity, hard won by my studies, before I may think of happiness. Forgive me, Devayani, and know that my suffering is doubled by the pain I unwillingly inflict on you.

Devayani: Forgiveness! You have angered my heart till it is hard and burning like a thunderbolt! You can go back to your work and your glory, but what is left for me? Memory is a bed of thorns, and secret shame will gnaw at the roots of my life. You came like a wayfarer, sat through the sunny hours in the shade of my garden, and to while time away you plucked all its flowers and wove them into a chain. And now, parting, you snap the thread and let the flowers drop on the dust! Accursed be that great knowledge you have earned!—a burden that, though others share equally with you, will never be lightened. For lack of love may it ever remain as foreign to your life as the cold stars are to the un-espoused darkness of virgin Night!

21

I "Why these preparations without end?"—I said to Mind—"Is some one to come?"

Mind replied, "I am enormously busy gathering things and building towers. I have no time to answer such questions."

Meekly I went back to my work.

When things were grown to a pile, when seven wings of his palace were complete, I said to Mind, "Is it not enough?"

Mind began to say, "Not enough to contain—" and then stopped.

"Contain what?" I asked.

Mind affected not to hear.

I suspected that Mind did not know, and with ceaseless work smothered the question.

His one refrain was, "I must have more."

"Why must you?"

"Because it is great."

"What is great?"

Mind remained silent. I pressed for an answer.

In contempt and anger, Mind said, "Why ask about things that are not? Take notice of those that are hugely before you,—the struggle and the fight, the army and armaments, the bricks and mortar, and labourers without number."

I thought "Possibly Mind is wise."

II Days passed. More wings were added to his palace—more lands to his domain.

The season of rains came to an end. The dark clouds became white and thin, and in the rain-washed sky the sunny hours hovered like butterflies over an unseen flower. I was bewildered and asked everybody I met, "What is that music in the breeze?"

A tramp walked the road whose dress was wild as his manner; he said, "Hark to the music of the Coming!"

I cannot tell why I was convinced, but the words broke from me, "We have not much longer to wait."

"It is close at hand," said the mad man.

I went to the office and boldly said to Mind, "Stop all work!"

Mind asked, "Have you any news?"

"Yes," I answered, "News of the Coming." But I could not explain.

Mind shook his head and said, "There are neither banners nor pageantry!"

III The night waned, the stars paled in the sky. Suddenly the touchstone of the morning light tinged everything with gold. A cry spread from mouth to mouth—

"Here is the herald!"

I bowed my head and asked, "Is he coming?"

The answer seemed to burst from all sides, "Yes."

Mind grew troubled and said, "The dome of my building is not yet finished, nothing is in order."

A voice came from the sky, "Pull down your building!"

"But why?" asked Mind.

"Because to-day is the day of the Coming, and your building is in the way."

IV The lofty building lies in the dust and all is scattered and broken.

Mind looked about. But what was there to see?

Only the morning star and the lily washed in dew.

And what else? A child running laughing from its mother's arms into the open light.

"Was it only for this that they said it was the day of the Coming?"

"Yes, this was why they said there was music in the air and light in the sky."

"And did they claim all the earth only for this?"

"Yes," came the answer. "Mind, you build walls to imprison yourself. Your servants toil to enslave themselves; but the whole earth and infinite space are for the child, for the New Life."

"What does that child bring you?"

"Hope for all the world and its joy."

Mind asked me, "Poet, do you understand?"

"I lay my work aside," I said, "for I must have time to understand."

22

TRANSLATIONS

VAISHNAVA SONGS

1 Oh Sakhi,[1] my sorrow knows no bounds.

[Footnote 1: The woman friend of a woman.]

August comes laden with rain clouds and my house is desolate.

The stormy sky growls, the earth is flooded with rain, my love is far away, and my heart is torn with anguish.

The peacocks dance, for the clouds rumble and frogs croak.

The night brims with darkness flicked with lightning.

Vidyapati[2] asks, "Maiden, how are you to spend your days and nights without your lord?"

2 Lucky was my awakening this morning, for I saw my beloved.

The sky was one piece of joy, and my life and youth were fulfilled.

To-day my house becomes my house in truth, and my body my body.

Fortune has proved a friend, and my doubts are dispelled.

Birds, sing your best; moon, shed your fairest light!

Let fly your darts, Love-God, in millions!

I wait for the moment when my body will grow golden at his touch.

Vidyapati says, "Immense is your good fortune, and blessed is your love."

---

2 The name of the poet.

3 I feel my body vanishing into the dust whereon my beloved walks.

I feel one with the water of the lake where he bathes.

Oh Sakhi, my love crosses death's boundary when I meet him.

My heart melts in the light and merges in the mirror whereby he views his face.

I move with the air to kiss him when he waves his fan, and wherever he wanders I enclose him like the sky.

Govindadas says, "You are the gold-setting, fair maiden, he is the emerald."

4 My love, I will keep you hidden in my eyes; I will thread your image like a gem on my joy and hang it on my bosom.

You have been in my heart ever since I was a child, throughout my youth, throughout my life, even through all my dreams.

You dwell in my being when I sleep and when I wake.

Know that I am a woman, and bear with me when you find me wanting.

For I have thought and thought and know for certain that all that is left for me in this world is your love, and if I lose you for a moment I die.

Chandidas says, "Be tender to her who is yours in life and death."

5 "Fruit to sell, Fruit to sell," cried the woman at the door.

The Child came out of the house.

"Give me some fruit," said he, putting a handful of rice in her basket.

The fruit-seller gazed at his face and her eyes swam with tears.

"Who is the fortunate mother," she cried, "that has clasped you in her arms and fed you at her breast, and whom your dear voice called 'Mother'?"

"Offer your fruit to him," says the poet, "and with it your life."

II

1

Endlessly varied art thou in the exuberant world, Lady of Manifold Magnificence. Thy path is strewn with lights, thy touch thrills into flowers; that trailing skirt of thine sweeps the whirl of a dance among the stars, and thy many-toned music is echoed from innumerable worlds through signs and colours.

Single and alone in the unfathomed stillness of the soul, art thou, Lady of Silence and Solitude, a vision thrilled with light, a lonely lotus blossoming on the stem of love.

2

Behind the rusty iron gratings of the opposite window sits a girl, dark and plain of face, like a boat stranded on a sand-bank when the river is shallow in the summer.

I come back to my room after my day's work, and my tired eyes are lured to her.

She seems to me like a lake with its dark lonely waters edged by moonlight.

She has only her window for freedom: there the morning light meets her musings, and through it her dark eyes like lost stars travel back to their sky.

3

I remember the day.

The heavy shower of rain is slackening into fitful pauses, renewed gusts of wind startle it from a first lull.

I take up my instrument. Idly I touch the strings, till, without my knowing, the music borrows the mad cadence of that storm.

I see her figure as she steals from her work, stops at my door, and retreats with hesitating steps. She comes again, stands outside leaning against the wall, then slowly enters the room and sits down. With head bent, she plies her needle in silence; but soon stops her work, and looks out of the window through the rain at the blurred line of trees.

Only this—one hour of a rainy noon filled with shadows and song and silence.

4

While stepping into the carriage she turned her head and threw me a swift glance of farewell.

This was her last gift to me. But where can I keep it safe from the trampling hours?

Must evening sweep this gleam of anguish away, as it will the last flicker of fire from the sunset?

Ought it to be washed off by the rain, as treasured pollens are from heart-broken flowers?

Leave kingly glory and the wealth of the rich to death. But may not tears keep ever fresh the memory of a glance flung through a passionate moment?

"Give it to me to keep," said my song; "I never touch kings' glory or the wealth of the rich, but these small things are mine for ever."

5

You give yourself to me, like a flower that blossoms at night, whose presence is known by the dew that drips from it, by the odour shed through the darkness, as the first steps of Spring are by the buds that thicken the twigs.

You break upon my thought like waves at the high tide, and my heart is drowned under surging songs.

My heart knew of your coming, as the night feels the approach of dawn. The clouds are aflame and my sky fills with a great revealing flood.

6

I was to go away; still she did not speak. But I felt, from a slight quiver, her yearning arms would say: "Ah no, not yet."

I have often heard her pleading hands vocal in a touch, though they knew not what they said.

I have known those arms to stammer when, had they not, they would have become youth's garland round my neck.

Their little gestures return to remembrance in the covert of still hours, like truants they playfully reveal things she had kept secret from me.

7

My songs are like bees; they follow through the air some fragrant trace—some memory—of you, to hum around your shyness, eager for its hidden store.

When the freshness of dawn droops in the sun, when in the noon the air hangs low with heaviness and the forest is silent, my songs return home, their languid wings dusted with gold.

8

I believe you had visited me in a vision before we ever met, like some foretaste of April before the spring broke into flower.

That vision must have come when all was bathed in the odour of *sal* blossom; when the twilight twinkle of the river fringed its yellow sands, and the vague sounds of a summer afternoon were blended; yes, and had it not laughed and evaded me in many a nameless gleam at other moments?

9

I think I shall stop startled if ever we meet after our next birth, walking in the light of a far-away world.

I shall know those dark eyes then as morning stars, and yet feel that they have belonged to some unremembered evening sky of a former life.

I shall know that the magic of your face is not all its own, but has stolen the passionate light that was in my eyes at some immemorial meeting, and then gathered from my love a mystery that has now forgotten its origin.

10

Lay down your lute, my love, leave your arms free to embrace me.

Let your touch bring my overflowing heart to my body's utmost brink.

Do not bend your neck and turn away your face, but offer up a kiss to me, which has been like some perfume long closed in a bud.

Do not smother this moment under vain words, but let our hearts quake in a rush of silence sweeping all thoughts to the shoreless delight.

11

You have made me great with your love, though I am but one among the many, drifting in the common tide, rocking in the fluctuant favour of the world.

You have given me a seat where poets of all time bring their tribute, and lovers with deathless names greet one another across the ages.

Men hastily pass me in the market,—never noting how my body has grown precious with your caress, how I carry your kiss within, as the sun carries in its orb the fire of the divine touch and shines for ever.

12

Like a child that frets and pushes away its toys, my heart to-day shakes its head at every phrase I suggest, and says, "No, not this."

Yet words, in the agony of their vagueness, haunt my mind, like vagrant clouds hovering over hills, waiting for some chance wind to relieve them of their rain.

But leave these vain efforts, my soul, for the stillness will ripen its own music in the dark.

My life to-day is like a cloister during some penance, where the spring is afraid to stir or to whisper.

This is not the time, my love, for you to pass the gate; at the mere thought of your anklet bells tinkling down the path, the garden echoes are ashamed.

Know that to-morrow's songs are in bud to-day, and should they see you walk by they would strain to breaking their immature hearts.

13

Whence do you bring this disquiet, my love?

Let my heart touch yours and kiss the pain out of your silence.

The night has thrown up from its depth this little hour, that love may build a new world within these shut doors, to be lighted by this solitary lamp.

We have for music but a single reed which our two pairs of lips must play on by turns—for crown, only one garland to bind my hair after I have put it on your forehead.

Tearing the veil from my breast I shall make our bed on the floor; and one kiss and one sleep of delight shall fill our small boundless world.

14

All that I had I gave to you, keeping but the barest veil of reserve.

It is so thin that you secretly smile at it and I feel ashamed.

The gust of the spring breeze sweeps it away unawares, and the flutter of my own heart moves it as the waves move their foam.

My love, do not grieve if I keep this flimsy mist of distance round me.

This frail reserve of mine is no mere woman's coyness, but a slender stem on which the flower of my self-surrender bends towards you with reticent grace.

15

I have donned this new robe to-day because my body feels like singing.

It is not enough that I am given to my love once and for ever, but out of that I must fashion new gifts every day; and shall I not seem a fresh offering, dressed in a new robe?

My heart, like the evening sky, has its endless passion for colour, and therefore I change my veils, which have now the green of the cool young grass and now that of the winter rice.

To-day my robe is tinted with the rain-rimmed blue of the sky. It brings to my limbs the colour of the boundless, the colour of the oversea hills; and it carries in its folds the delight of summer clouds flying in the wind.

16

I thought I would write love's words in their own colour; but that lies deep in the heart, and tears are pale.

Would you know them, friend, if the words were colourless?

I thought I would sing love's words to their own tune, but that sounds only in my heart, and my eyes are silent.

Would you know them, friend, if there were no tune?

17

In the night the song came to me; but you were not there.

It found the words for which I had been seeking all day. Yes, in the stillness a moment after dark they throbbed into music, even as the stars then began to pulse with light; but you were not there. My hope was to sing it to you in the morning; but, try as I might, though the music came, the words hung back, when you were beside me.

18

The night deepens and the dying flame flickers in the lamp.

I forgot to notice when the evening—like a village girl who has filled her pitcher at the river a last time for that day—closed the door on her cabin.

I was speaking to you, my love, with mind barely conscious of my voice—tell me, had it any meaning? Did it bring you any message from beyond life's borders?

For now, since my voice has ceased, I feel the night throbbing with thoughts that gaze in awe at the abyss of their dumbness.

19

When we two first met my heart rang out in music, "She who is eternally afar is beside you for ever."

That music is silent, because I have grown to believe that my love is only near, and have forgotten that she is also far, far away.

Music fills the infinite between two souls. This has been muffled by the mist of our daily habits.

On shy summer nights, when the breeze brings a vast murmur out of the silence, I sit up in my bed and mourn the great loss of her who is beside me. I ask myself, "When shall I have another chance to whisper to her words with the rhythm of eternity in them?"

Wake up, my song, from thy languor, rend this screen of the familiar, and fly to my beloved there, in the endless surprise of our first meeting!

20

Lovers come to you, my Queen, and proudly lay their riches at your feet: but my tribute is made up of unfulfilled hopes.

Shadows have stolen across the heart of my world and the best in me has lost light.

While the fortunate laugh at my penury, I ask you to lend my failings your tears, and so make them precious.

I bring you a voiceless instrument.

I strained to reach a note which was too high in my heart, and the string broke.

While masters laugh at the snapped cord, I ask you to take my lute in your hands and fill its hollowness with your songs.

21

The father came back from the funeral rites.

His boy of seven stood at the window, with eyes wide open and a golden amulet hanging from his neck, full of thoughts too difficult for his age.

His father took him in his arms and the boy asked him, "Where is mother?"

"In heaven," answered his father, pointing to the sky.

At night the father groaned in slumber, weary with grief.

A lamp dimly burned near the bedroom door, and a lizard chased moths on the wall.

The boy woke up from sleep, felt with his hands the emptiness in the bed, and stole out to the open terrace.

The boy raised his eyes to the sky and long gazed in silence. His bewildered mind sent abroad into the night the question, "Where is heaven?"

No answer came: and the stars seemed like the burning tears of that ignorant darkness.

22

She went away when the night was about to wane.

My mind tried to console me by saying, "All is vanity."

I felt angry and said, "That unopened letter with her name on it, and this palm-leaf fan bordered with red silk by her own hands, are they not real?"

The day passed, and my friend came and said to me, "Whatever is good is true, and can never perish."

"How do you know?" I asked impatiently; "was not this body good which is now lost to the world?"

As a fretful child hurting its own mother, I tried to wreck all the shelters that ever I had, in and about me, and cried, "This world is treacherous."

Suddenly I felt a voice saying—"Ungrateful!"

I looked out of the window, and a reproach seemed to come from the star-sprinkled night,–"You pour out into the void of my absence your faith in the truth that I came!"

23

The river is grey and the air dazed with blown sand.

On a morning of dark disquiet, when the birds are mute and their nests shake in the gust, I sit alone and ask myself, "Where is she?"

The days have flown wherein we sat too near each other; we laughed and jested, and the awe of love's majesty found no words at our meetings.

I made myself small, and she trifled away every moment with pelting talk.

To-day I wish in vain that she were by me, in the gloom of the coming storm, to sit in the soul's solitude.

24

The name she called me by, like a flourishing jasmine, covered the whole seventeen years of our love. With its sound mingled the quiver of the light through the leaves, the scent of the grass in the rainy night, and the sad silence of the last hour of many an idle day.

Not the work of God alone was he who answered to that name; she created him again for herself during those seventeen swift years.

Other years were to follow, but their vagrant days, no longer gathered within the fold of that name uttered in her voice, stray and are scattered.

They ask me, "Who should fold us?"

I find no answer and sit silent, and they cry to me while dispersing, "We seek a shepherdess!"

Whom should they seek?

That they do not know. And like derelict evening clouds they drift in the trackless dark, and are lost and forgotten.

25

I feel that your brief days of love have not been left behind in those scanty years of your life.

I seek to know in what place, away from the slow-thieving dust, you keep them now. I find in my solitude some song of your evening that died, yet left a deathless echo; and the sighs of your unsatisfied hours I find nestled in the warm quiet of the autumn noon.

Your desires come from the hive of the past to haunt my heart, and I sit still to listen to their wings.

26

You have taken a bath in the dark sea. You are once again veiled in a bride's robe, and through death's arch you come back to repeat our wedding in the soul.

Neither lute nor drum is struck, no crowd has gathered, not a wreath is hung on the gate.

Your unuttered words meet mine in a ritual unillumined by lamps.

27

I was walking along a path overgrown with grass, when suddenly I heard from some one behind, "See if you know me?"

I turned round and looked at her and said, "I cannot remember your name."

She said, "I am that first great Sorrow whom you met when you were young."

Her eyes looked like a morning whose dew is still in the air.

I stood silent for some time till I said, "Have you lost all the great burden of your tears?"

She smiled and said nothing. I felt that her tears had had time to learn the language of smiles.

"Once you said," she whispered, "that you would cherish your grief for ever."

I blushed and said, "Yes, but years have passed and I forget."

Then I took her hand in mine and said, "But you have changed."

"What was sorrow once has now become peace," she said.

28

Our life sails on the uncrossed sea whose waves chase each other in an eternal hide-and-seek.

It is the restless sea of change, feeding its foaming flocks to lose them over and over again, beating its hands against the calm of the sky.

Love, in the centre of this circling war-dance of light and dark, yours is that green island, where the sun kisses the shy forest shade and silence is wooed by birds' singing.

29

AMA AND VINAYAKA

Night on the battlefield: AMA *meets her father* VINAYAKA.

Ama: Father!

Vinayaka: Shameless wanton, you call me "Father"! you who did not shrink from a Mussulman husband!

Ama: Though you have treacherously killed my husband, yet you are my father; and I hold back a widow's tears, lest they bring God's curse on you. Since we have met on this battlefield after years of separation, let me bow to your feet and take my last leave!

Vinayaka: Where will you go, Ama? The tree on which you built your impious nest is hewn down. Where will *you* take shelter?

Ama: I have my son.

Vinayaka: Leave him! Cast never a fond look back on the result of a sin expiated with blood! Think where to go.

Ama: Death's open gates are wider than a father's love!

Vinayaka: Death indeed swallows sins as the sea swallows the mud of rivers. But you are to die neither to-night nor here. Seek some solitary shrine of holy Shiva far from shamed kindred and all neighbours; bathe three times a day in sacred Ganges, and, while reciting God's name, listen to the last bell of evening worship, that Death may look tenderly upon you, as a father on his sleeping child whose eyes are still wet with tears. Let him gently carry you into his own great silence, as the Ganges carries a fallen flower on its stream, washing every stain away to render it, a fit offering, to the sea.

Ama: But my son——

Vinayaka: Again I bid you not to speak of him. Lay yourself once more in a father's arms, my child, like a babe fresh from the womb of Oblivion, your second mother.

Ama: To me the world has become a shadow. Your words I hear, but cannot take to heart. Leave me, father, leave me alone! Do not try to bind me with your love, for its bands are red with my husband's blood.

Vinayaka: Alas! no flower ever returns to the parent branch it dropped from. How can you call him *husband* who forcibly snatched you from Jivaji to whom you had been sacredly affianced? I shall never forget that night! In the wedding hall we sat anxiously expecting the bridegroom, for the auspicious hour was dwindling away. Then in the distance appeared the glare of torches, and bridal strains came floating up the air. We shouted for joy: women blew their conch-shells. A procession of palanquins entered the courtyard: but while we were asking, «Where is Jivaji?» armed men burst out of the litters like a storm, and bore you off before we knew what had happened. Shortly after, Jivaji came to tell us he had been waylaid and captured by a Mussulman noble of the Vijapur court. That night Jivaji and I touched the nuptial fire and swore bloody death to this villain. After waiting long, we have been freed from our solemn pledge to-night; and the spirit of Jivaji, who lost his life in this battle, lawfully claims you for wife.

Ama: Father, it may be that I have disgraced the rites of your house, but my honour is unsullied; I loved him to whom I bore a son. I remember the night when I received two secret messages, one from you, one from my mother; yours said: "I send you the knife; kill him!" My mother's: "I send you the poison; end your life!" Had unholy force dishonoured me, your double bidding had been obeyed. But my body was yielded only after love had given *me*—love all the greater, all the purer, in that it overcame the hereditary recoil of our blood from the Mussulman.

Enter RAMA, AMA›S *mother*

Ama: Mother mine, I had not hoped to see you again. Let me take dust from your feet.

Rama: Touch me not with impure hands!

Ama: I am as pure as yourself.

Rama: To whom have you surrendered your honour?

Ama: To my husband.

Rama: Husband? A Mussulman the husband of a Brahmin woman?

Ama: I do not merit contempt: I am proud to say I never despised my husband though a Mussulman. If Paradise will reward your devotion to your husband, then the same Paradise waits for your daughter, who has been as true a wife.

Rama: Are you indeed a true wife?

Ama: Yes.

Rama: Do you know how to die without flinching?

Ama: I do.

Rama: Then let the funeral fire be lighted for you! See, there lies the body of your husband.

Ama: Jivaji?

Rama: Yes, Jivaji. He was your husband by plighted troth. The baffled fire of the nuptial God has raged into the hungry fire of death, and the interrupted wedding shall be completed now.

Vinayaka: Do not listen, my child. Go back to your son, to your own nest darkened with sorrow. My duty has been performed to its extreme cruel end, and nothing now remains for you to do.—Wife, your grief is fruitless. Were the branch dead which was violently snapped from our tree, I should give it to the fire. But it has sent living roots into a new soil and is bearing flowers and fruits. Allow her, without regret, to obey the laws of those among whom she has loved. Come, wife, it is time we cut all worldly ties and spent our remainder lives in the seclusion of some peaceful pilgrim shrine.

Rama: I am ready: but first must tread into dust every sprout of sin and shame that has sprung from the soil of our life. A daughter's infamy stains her mother's honour. That black shame shall feed glowing fire to-night, and raise a true wife's memorial over the ashes of my daughter.

Ama: Mother, if by force you unite me in death with one who was not my husband, then will you bring a curse upon yourself for desecrating the shrine of the Eternal Lord of Death.

Rama: Soldiers, light the fire; surround the woman!

Ama: Father!

Vinayaka: Do not fear. Alas, my child, that you should ever have to call your father to save you from your mother's hands!

Ama: Father!

Vinayaka: Come to me, my darling child! Mere vanity are these man-made laws, splashing like spray against the rock of heaven's ordinance. Bring your son to me, and we will live together, my daughter. A father's love, like God's rain, does not judge but is poured forth from an abounding source.

Rama: Where would you go? Turn back!—Soldiers, stand firm in your loyalty to your master Jivaji! do your last sacred duty by him!

Ama: Father!

Vinayaka: Free her, soldiers! She is my daughter.

Soldiers:	She is the widow of our master.
Vinayaka:	Her husband, though a Mussulman, was staunch in his own faith.
Rama:	Soldiers, keep this old man under control!
Ama:	I defy you, mother!–You, soldiers, I defy!–for through death and love I win to freedom.

30

A painter was selling pictures at the fair; followed by servants, there passed the son of a minister who in youth had cheated this painter's father so that he had died of a broken heart.

The boy lingered before the pictures and chose one for himself. The painter flung a cloth over it and said he would not sell it.

After this the boy pined heart-sick till his father came and offered a large price. But the painter kept the picture unsold on his shop-wall and grimly sat before it, saying to himself, "This is my revenge."

The sole form this painter's worship took was to trace an image of his god every morning.

And now he felt these pictures grow daily more different from those he used to paint.

This troubled him, and he sought in vain for an explanation till one day he started up from work in horror, the eyes of the god he had just drawn were those of the minister, and so were the lips.

He tore up the picture, crying, "My revenge has returned on my head!"

31

The General came before the silent and angry King and saluting him said: "The village is punished, the men are stricken to dust, and the women cower in their unlit homes afraid to weep aloud."

The High Priest stood up and blessed the King and cried: "God's mercy is ever upon you."

The Clown, when he heard this, burst out laughing and startled the court. The King's frown darkened.

"The honour of the throne," said the minister, "is upheld by the King's prowess and the blessing of Almighty God."

Louder laughed the Clown, and the King growled,–"Unseemly mirth!"

"God has showered many blessings upon your head," said the Clown; "the one he bestowed on me was the gift of laughter."

"This gift will cost you your life," said the King, gripping his sword with his right hand.

Yet the Clown stood up and laughed till he laughed no more.

A shadow of dread fell upon the Court, for they heard that laughter echoing in the depth of God's silence.

32

THE MOTHER'S PRAYER

Prince Duryodhana, the son of the blind Kaurava King Dhritarashtra, and of Queen Gandhari, has played with his cousins the Pandava Kings for their kingdom, and won it by fraud.

Dhritarashtra: You have compassed your end.

Duryodhana: Success is mine!

Dhritarashtra: Are you happy?

Duryodhana: I am victorious.

Dhritarashtra: I ask you again, what happiness have you in winning the undivided kingdom?

Duryodhana: Sire, a Kshatriya thirsts not after happiness but victory, that fiery wine pressed from seething jealousy. Wretchedly happy we were, like those inglorious stains that lie idly on the breast of the moon, when we lived in peace under the friendly dominance of our cousins. Then these Pandavas milked the world of its wealth, and allowed us a share, in brotherly tolerance. Now that they own defeat and expect banishment, I am no longer happy but exultant.

Dhritarashtra: Wretch, you forget that both Pandavas and Kauravas have the same forefathers.

Duryodhana: It was difficult to forget that, and therefore our inequalities rankled in my heart.

At midnight the moon is never jealous of the noonday sun. But the struggle to share one horizon between both orbs cannot last forever. Thank heaven, that struggle is over, and we have at last won solitude in glory.

Dhritarashtra: The mean jealousy!

Duryodhana: Jealousy is never mean—it is in the essence of greatness. Grass can grow in crowded amity, not giant trees. Stars live in clusters, but the sun and moon are lonely in their splendour. The pale moon of the Pandavas sets behind the forest shadows, leaving the new-risen sun of the Kauravas to rejoice.

Dhritarashtra: But right has been defeated.

Duryodhana: Right for rulers is not what is right in the eyes of the people. The people thrive by comradeship: but for a king, equals are enemies. They are obstacles ahead, they are terrors from behind. There is no place for brothers or friends in a king's polity; its one solid foundation is conquest.

Dhritarashtra: I refuse to call a conquest what was won by fraud in gambling.

Duryodhana: A man is not shamed by refusing to challenge a tiger on equal terms with teeth and nails. Our weapons are those proper for success, not for suicide. Father, I am proud of the result and disdain regret for the means.

Dhritarashtra: But justice——

Duryodhana: Fools alone dream of justice–success is not yet theirs: but those born to rule rely on power, merciless and unhampered with scruples.

Dhritarashtra: Your success will bring down on you a loud and angry flood of detraction.

Duryodhana: The people will take amazingly little time to learn that Duryodhana is king and has power to crush calumny under foot.

Dhritarashtra: Calumny dies of weariness dancing on tongue-tips. Do not drive it into the heart to gather strength.

Duryodhana: Unuttered defamation does not touch a king's dignity. I care not if love is refused us, but insolence shall not be borne. Love depends upon the will of the giver, and the poorest of the poor can indulge in such generosity. Let them squander it on their pet cats, tame dogs, and our good cousins the Pandavas. I shall never envy them. Fear is the tribute I claim for my royal throne. Father, only too leniently you lent your ear to those who slandered your sons: but if you intend still to allow those pious friends of yours to revel in shrill denunciation at the expense of your children, let us exchange our kingdom for the exile of our cousins, and go to the wilderness, where happily friends are never cheap!

Dhritarashtra: Could the pious warnings of my friends lessen my love for my sons, then we might be saved. But I have dipped my hands in the mire of your infamy and lost my sense of goodness. For your sakes I have heedlessly set fire to the ancient forest of our royal lineage—so dire is my love. Clasped breast to breast, we, like a double meteor, are blindly plunging into ruin. Therefore doubt not my love; relax not your embrace till the brink of annihilation be reached. Beat your drums of victory, lift your banner of triumph. In this mad riot of exultant evil, brothers and friends will disperse till nothing remain save the doomed father, the doomed son and God's curse.

Enter an Attendant

Sire, Queen Gandhari asks for audience.

Dhritarashtra: I await her.

Duryodhana: Let me take my leave. [*Exit.*

Dhritarashtra: Fly! For you cannot bear the fire of your mother's presence.

Enter QUEEN GANDHARI, *the mother of* DURYODHANA

Gandhari:	At your feet I crave a boon.
Dhritarashtra:	Speak, your wish is fulfilled.
Gandhari:	The time has come to renounce him.
Dhritarashtra:	Whom, my queen?
Gandhari:	Duryodhana!
Dhritarashtra:	Our own son, Duryodhana?
Gandhari:	Yes!
Dhritarashtra:	This is a terrible boon for you, his mother, to crave!
Gandhari:	The fathers of the Kauravas, who are in Paradise, join me in beseeching you.
Dhritarashtra:	The divine Judge will punish him who has broken His laws. But I am his father.
Gandhari:	Am I not his mother? Have I not carried him under my throbbing heart? Yes, I ask you to renounce Duryodhana the unrighteous.
Dhritarashtra:	What will remain to us after that?
Gandhari:	God's blessing.
Dhritarashtra:	And what will that bring us?
Gandhari:	New afflictions. Pleasure in our son's presence, pride in a new kingdom, and shame

at knowing both purchased by wrong done or connived at, like thorns dragged two ways, would lacerate our bosoms. The Pandavas are too proud ever to accept back from us the lands which they have relinquished; therefore it is only meet that we draw some great sorrow down on our heads so as to deprive that unmerited reward of its sting.

Dhritarashtra: Queen, you inflict fresh pain on a heart already rent.

Gandhari: Sire, the punishment imposed on our son will be more ours than his. A judge callous to the pain that he inflicts loses the right to judge. And if you spare your son to save yourself pain, then all the culprits ever punished by your hands will cry before God's throne for vengeance,—had they not also their fathers?

Dhritarashtra: No more of this, Queen, I pray you. Our son is abandoned of God: that is why I cannot give him up. To save him is no longer in my power, and therefore my consolation is to share his guilt and tread the path of destruction, his solitary companion. What is done is done; let follow what must follow! [*Exit.*

Gandhari: Be calm, my heart, and patiently await God's judgment. Oblivious night wears on, the morning of reckoning nears, I hear the thundering roar of its chariot. Woman, bow your head down to the dust! and as a sacrifice fling your heart under those wheels! Darkness will shroud the sky, earth will tremble, wailing will rend the air and then comes the silent and cruel end,—that terrible peace, that great forgetting, and awful extinction of hatred—the supreme deliverance rising from the fire of death.

33

Fiercely they rend in pieces the carpet woven during ages of prayer for the welcome of the world's best hope.

The great preparations of love lie a heap of shreds, and there is nothing on the ruined altar to remind the mad crowd that their god was to have come. In a fury of passion they seem to have burnt their future to cinders, and with it the season of their bloom.

The air is harsh with the cry, "Victory to the Brute!" The children look haggard and aged; they whisper to one another that time revolves but never advances, that we are goaded to run but have nothing to reach, that creation is like a blind man's groping.

I said to myself, "Cease thy singing. Song is for one who is to come, the struggle without an end is for things that are."

The road, that ever lies along like some one with ear to the ground listening for footsteps, to-day gleans no hint of coming guest, nothing of the house at its far end.

My lute said, "Trample me in the dust."

I looked at the dust by the roadside. There was a tiny flower among thorns. And I cried, "The world's hope is not dead!"

The sky stooped over the horizon to whisper to the earth, and a hush of expectation filled the air. I saw the palm leaves clapping their hands to the beat of inaudible music, and the moon exchanged glances with the glistening silence of the lake.

The road said to me, "Fear nothing!" and my lute said, "Lend me thy songs!"

34

TRANSLATIONS

BAUL SONGS[3]

1

This longing to meet in the play of love, my Lover, is not only mine but yours.

Your lips can smile, your flute make music, only through delight in my love; therefore you are importunate even as I.

2

I sit here on the road; do not ask me to walk further.

If your love can be complete without mine let me turn back from seeking you.

I refuse to beg a sight of you if you do not feel my need.

3 The Bauls are a sect of religious mendicants in Bengal, unlettered and unconventional, whose songs are loved and sung by the people. The literal meaning of the word "Baul" is "the Mad."

I am blind with market dust and mid-day glare, and so wait, in hopes that your heart, my heart's lover, will send you to find me.

3

I am poured forth in living notes of joy and sorrow by your breath.

Mornings and evenings in summer and in rains, I am fashioned to music.

Should I be wholly spent in some flight of song, I shall not grieve, the tune is so dear to me.

4

My heart is a flute he has played on. If ever it fall into other hands let him fling it away.

My lover's flute is dear to him, therefore if to-day alien breath have entered it and sounded strange notes, let him break it to pieces and strew the dust with them.

5

In love the aim is neither pain nor pleasure but love only.

While free love binds, division destroys it, for love is what unites.

Love is lit from love as fire from fire, but whence came the first flame?

In your being it leaps under the rod of pain.

Then, when the hidden fire flames forth, the in and the out are one and all barriers fall in ashes.

Let the pain glow fiercely, burst from the heart and beat back darkness, need you be afraid?

The poet says, "Who can buy love without paying its price? When you fail to give yourself you make the whole world miserly."

6

Eyes see only dust and earth, but feel with the heart, and know pure joy.

The delights blossom on all sides in every form, but where is your heart's thread to make a wreath of them?

My master's flute sounds through all things, drawing me out of my lodgings wherever they may be, and while I listen I know that every step I take is in my master's house.

For he is the sea, he is the river that leads to the sea, and he is the landing-place.

7

Strange ways has my guest.

He comes at times when I am unprepared, yet how can I refuse him?

I watch all night with lighted lamp; he stays away; when the light goes out and the room is bare he comes claiming his seat, and can I keep him waiting?

I laugh and make merry with friends, then suddenly I start up, for lo! he passes me by in sorrow, and I know my mirth was vain.

I have often seen a smile in his eyes when my heart ached, then I knew my sorrow was not real.

Yet I never complain when I do not understand him.

8

I am the boat, you are the sea, and also the boatman.

Though you never make the shore, though you let me sink, why should I be foolish and afraid?

Is reaching the shore a greater prize than losing myself with you?

If you are only the haven, as they say, then what is the sea?

Let it surge and toss me on its waves, I shall be content.

I live in you whatever and however you appear. Save me or kill me as you wish, only never leave me in other hands.

9

Make way, O bud, make way, burst open thy heart and make way.

The opening spirit has overtaken thee, canst thou remain a bud any longer?

III

1

Come, Spring, reckless lover of the earth, make the forest's heart pant for utterance!

Come in gusts of disquiet where flowers break open and jostle the new leaves!

Burst, like a rebellion of light, through the night's vigil, through the lake's dark dumbness, through the dungeon under the dust, proclaiming freedom to the shackled seeds!

Like the laughter of lightning, like the shout of a storm, break into the midst of the noisy town; free stifled word and unconscious effort, reinforce our flagging fight, and conquer death!

2

I have looked on this picture in many a month of March when the mustard is in bloom—this lazy line of the water and the grey of the sand beyond, the rough path along the river-bank carrying the comradeship of the field into the heart of the village.

I have tried to capture in rhyme the idle whistle of the wind, the beat of the oar-strokes from a passing boat.

I have wondered in my mind how simply it stands before me, this great world: with what fond and familiar ease it fills my heart, this encounter with the Eternal Stranger.

3

The ferry-boat plies between the two villages facing each other across the narrow stream.

The water is neither wide nor deep—a mere break in the path that enhances the small adventures of daily life, like a break in the words of a song across which the tune gleefully streams.

While the towers of wealth rise high and crash to ruin, these villages talk to each other across the garrulous stream, and the ferry-boat plies between them, age after age, from seed-time to harvest.

4

In the evening after they have brought their cattle home, they sit on the grass before their huts to know that you are among them unseen, to repeat in their songs the name which they have fondly given you.

While kings' crowns shine and disappear like falling stars, around village huts your name rises through the still night from the simple hearts of your lovers whose names are unrecorded.

5

In Baby's world, the trees shake their leaves at him, murmuring verses in an ancient tongue that dates from before the age of meaning, and the moon feigns to be of his own age—the solitary baby of night.

In the world of the old, flowers dutifully blush at the make-believe of faery legends, and broken dolls confess that they are made of clay.

6

My world, when I was a child, you were a little girl-neighbour, a loving timid stranger.

Then you grew bold and talked to me across the fence, offering me toys and flowers and shells.

Next you coaxed me away from my work, you tempted me into the land of the dusk or the weedy corner of some garden in mid-day loneliness.

At length you told me stories about bygone times, with which the present ever longs to meet so as to be rescued from its prison in the moment.

7

How often, great Earth, have I felt my being yearn to flow over you, sharing in the happiness of each green blade that raises its signal banner in answer to the beckoning blue of the sky!

I feel as if I had belonged to you ages before I was born. That is why, in the days when the autumn light shimmers on the mellowing ears of rice, I seem to remember a past when my mind was everywhere, and even to hear voices as of playfellows echoing from the remote and deeply veiled past.

When, in the evening, the cattle return to their folds, raising dust from the meadow paths, as the moon rises higher than the smoke ascending from the village huts, I feel sad as for some great separation that happened in the first morning of existence.

8

My mind still buzzed with the cares of a busy day; I sat on without noting how twilight was deepening into dark. Suddenly light stirred across the gloom and touched me as with a finger.

I lifted my head and met the gaze of the full moon widened in wonder like a child's. It held my eyes for long, and I felt as though a love-letter had been secretly dropped in at my window. And ever since my heart is breaking to write for answer something fragrant as Night's unseen flowers—great as her declaration spelt out in nameless stars.

9

The clouds thicken till the morning light seems like a bedraggled fringe to the rainy night.

A little girl stands at her window, still as a rainbow at the gate of a broken-down storm.

She is my neighbour, and has come upon the earth like some god's rebellious laughter. Her mother in anger calls her incorrigible; her father smiles and calls her mad.

She is like a runaway waterfall leaping over boulders, like the topmost bamboo twig rustling in the restless wind.

She stands at her window looking out into the sky.

Her sister comes to say, "Mother calls you." She shakes her head.

Her little brother with his toy boat comes and tries to pull her off to play; she snatches her hand from his. The boy persists and she gives him a slap on the back.

The first great voice was the voice of wind and water in the beginning of earth's creation.

That ancient cry of nature—her dumb call to unborn life—has reached this child's heart and leads it out alone beyond the fence of our times: so there she stands, possessed by eternity!

10

The kingfisher sits still on the prow of an empty boat, while in the shallow margin of the stream a buffalo lies tranquilly blissful, its eyes half closed to savour the luxury of cool mud.

Undismayed by the barking of the village cur, the cow browses on the bank, followed by a hopping group of *saliks* hunting moths.

I sit in the tamarind grove, where the cries of dumb life congregate—the cattle's lowing, the sparrows' chatter, the shrill scream of a kite overhead, the crickets' chirp, and the splash of a fish in the water.

I peep into the primeval nursery of life, where the mother Earth thrills at the first living clutch near her breast.

11

At the sleepy village the noon was still like a sunny midnight when my holidays came to their end.

My little girl of four had followed me all the morning from room to room, watching my preparations in grave silence, till, wearied, she sat by the doorpost strangely quiet, murmuring to herself, "Father must not go!"

This was the meal hour, when sleep daily overcame her, but her mother had forgotten her and the child was too unhappy to complain.

At last, when I stretched out my arms to her to say farewell, she never moved, but sadly looking at me said, "Father, you must not go!"

And it amused me to tears to think how this little child dared to fight the giant world of necessity with no other resource than those few words, "Father, you must not go!"

12

Take your holiday, my boy; there are the blue sky and the bare field, the barn and the ruined temple under the ancient tamarind.

My holiday must be taken through yours, finding light in the dance of your eyes, music in your noisy shouts.

To you autumn brings the true holiday freedom: to me it brings the impossibility of work; for lo! you burst into my room.

Yes, my holiday is an endless freedom for love to disturb me.

13

In the evening my little daughter heard a call from her companions below the window.

She timidly went down the dark stairs holding a lamp in her hand, shielding it behind her veil.

I was sitting on my terrace in the star-lit night of March, when at a sudden cry I ran to see.

Her lamp had gone out in the dark spiral staircase. I asked, "Child, why did you cry?"

From below she answered in distress, "Father, I have lost my-self!"

When I came back to the terrace under the star-lit night of March, I looked at the sky, and it seemed that a child was walking there treasuring many lamps behind her veils.

If their light went out, she would suddenly stop and a cry would sound from sky to sky, "Father, I have lost myself!"

14

The evening stood bewildered among street lamps, its gold tarnished by the city dust.

A woman, gaudily decked and painted, leant over the rail of her balcony, a living fire waiting for its moths.

Suddenly an eddy was formed in the road round a street-boy crushed under the wheels of a carriage, and the woman on the balcony fell to the floor screaming in agony, stricken with the grief of the great white-robed Mother who sits in the world's inner shrine.

15

I remember the scene on the barren heath—a girl sat alone on the grass before the gipsy camp, braiding her hair in the afternoon shade.

Her little dog jumped and barked at her busy hands, as though her employment had no importance.

In vain did she rebuke it, calling it "a pest," saying she was tired of its perpetual silliness.

She struck it on the nose with her reproving forefinger, which only seemed to delight it the more.

She looked menacingly grave for a few moments, to warn it of impending doom; and then, letting her hair fall, quickly snatched it up in her arms, laughed, and pressed it to her heart.

16

He is tall and lean, withered to the bone with long repeated fever, like a dead tree unable to draw a single drop of sap from anywhere.

In despairing patience, his mother carries him like a child into the sun, where he sits by the roadside in the shortening shadows of each forenoon.

The world passes by—a woman to fetch water, a herd-boy with cattle to pasture, a laden cart to the distant market—and the mother hopes that some least stir of life may touch the awful torpor of her dying son.

17

If the ragged villager, trudging home from the market, could suddenly be lifted to the crest of a distant age, men would stop in their work and shout and run to him in delight.

For they would no longer whittle down the man into the peasant, but find him full of the mystery and spirit of his age.

Even his poverty and pain would grow great, released from the shallow insult of the present, and the paltry things in his basket would acquire pathetic dignity.

18

With the morning he came out to walk a road shaded by a file of deodars, that coiled the hill round like importunate love.

He held the first letter from his newly wedded wife in their village home, begging him to come to her, and come soon.

The touch of an absent hand haunted him as he walked, and the air seemed to take up the cry of the letter: "Love, my love, my sky is brimming with tears!"

He asked himself in wonder, "How do I deserve this?"

The sun suddenly appeared over the rim of the blue hills, and four girls from a foreign shore came with swift strides, talking loud and followed by a barking dog.

The two elder turned away to conceal their amusement at something strange in his insignificance, and the younger ones pushed each other, laughed aloud, and ran off in exuberant mirth.

He stopped and his head sank. Then he suddenly felt his letter, opened and read it again.

19

The day came for the image from the temple to be drawn round the holy town in its chariot.

The Queen said to the King, "Let us go and attend the festival."

Only one man out of the whole household did not join in the pilgrimage. His work was to collect stalks of spear-grass to make brooms for the King's house.

The chief of the servants said in pity to him, "You may come with us."

He bowed his head, saying, "It cannot be."

The man dwelt by the road along which the King's followers had to pass. And when the Minister's elephant reached this spot, he called to him and said, "Come with us and see the God ride in his chariot!"

"I dare not seek God after the King's fashion," said the man.

"How should you ever have such luck again as to see the God in his chariot?" asked the Minister.

"When God himself comes to my door," answered the man.

The Minister laughed loud and said, "Fool! 'When God comes to your door!' yet a King must travel to see him!"

"Who except God visits the poor?" said the man.

20

Days were drawing out as the winter ended, and, in the sun, my dog played in his wild way with the pet deer.

The crowd going to the market gathered by the fence, and laughed to see the love of these playmates struggle with languages so dissimilar.

The spring was in the air, and the young leaves fluttered like flames. A gleam danced in the deer's dark eyes when she started, bent her neck at the movement of her own shadow, or raised her ears to listen to some whisper in the wind.

The message comes floating with the errant breeze, with the rustle and glimmer abroad in the April sky. It sings of the first ache of youth in the world, when the first flower broke from the bud, and love went forth seeking that which it knew not, leaving all it had known.

And one afternoon, when among the *amlak* trees the shadow grew grave and sweet with the furtive caress of light, the deer set off to run like a meteor in love with death.

It grew dark, and lamps were lighted in the house; the stars came out and night was upon the fields, but the deer never came back.

My dog ran up to me whining, questioning me with his piteous eyes which seemed to say, "I do not understand!"

But who does ever understand?

21

Our Lane is tortuous, as if, ages ago, she started in quest of her goal, vacillated right and left, and remained bewildered for ever.

Above in the air, between her buildings, hangs like a ribbon a strip torn out of space: she calls it her sister of the blue town.

She sees the sun only for a few moments at mid-day, and asks herself in wise doubt, "Is it real?"

In June rain sometimes shades her band of daylight as with pencil hatchings. The path grows slippery with mud, and umbrellas collide. Sudden jets of water from spouts overhead splash on her startled pavement. In her dismay, she takes it for the jest of an unmannerly scheme of creation.

The spring breeze, gone astray in her coil of contortions, stumbles like a drunken vagabond against angle and corner, filling the dusty air with scraps of paper and rag. "What fury of foolishness! Are the Gods gone mad?" she exclaims in indignation.

But the daily refuse from the houses on both sides—scales of fish mixed with ashes, vegetable peelings, rotten fruit, and dead rats—never rouse her to question, "Why should these things be?"

She accepts every stone of her paving. But from between their chinks sometimes a blade of grass peeps up. That baffles her. How can solid facts permit such intrusion?

On a morning when at the touch of autumn light her houses wake up into beauty from their foul dreams, she whispers to herself, "There is a limitless wonder somewhere beyond these buildings."

But the hours pass on; the households are astir; the maid strolls back from the market, swinging her right arm and with the left clasping the basket of provisions to her side; the air grows thick with the smell and smoke of kitchens. It again becomes clear to our Lane that the real and normal consist solely of herself, her houses, and their muck-heaps.

22

The house, lingering on after its wealth has vanished, stands by the wayside like a madman with a patched rag over his back.

Day after day scars it with spiteful scratches, and rainy months leave their fantastic signatures on its bared bricks.

In a deserted upper room one of a pair of doors has fallen from rusty hinges; and the other, widowed, bangs day and night to the fitful gusts.

One night the sound of women wailing came from that house. They mourned the death of the last son of the family, a boy of eighteen, who earned his living by playing the part of the heroine in a travelling theatre.

A few days more and the house became silent, and all the doors were locked.

Only on the north side in the upper room that desolate door would neither drop off to its rest nor be shut, but swung to and fro in the wind like a self-torturing soul.

After a time children's voices echo once more through that house. Over the balcony-rail women's clothes are hung in the sun, a bird whistles from a covered cage, and a boy plays with his kite on the terrace.

A tenant has come to occupy a few rooms. He earns little and has many children. The tired mother beats them and they roll on the floor and shriek.

A maid-servant of forty drudges through the day, quarrels with her mistress, threatens to, but never leaves.

Every day some small repairs are done. Paper is pasted in place of missing panes; gaps in the railings are made good with split bamboo; an empty box keeps the boltless gate shut; old stains vaguely show through new whitewash on the walls.

The magnificence of wealth had found a fitting memorial in gaunt desolation; but, lacking sufficient means, they try to hide this with dubious devices, and its dignity is outraged.

They have overlooked the deserted room on the north side. And its forlorn door still bangs in the wind, like Despair beating her breast.

23

In the depths of the forest the ascetic practised penance with fast-closed eyes; he intended to deserve Paradise.

But the girl who gathered twigs brought him fruits in her skirt, and water from the stream in cups made of leaves.

The days went on, and his penance grew harsher till the fruits remained untasted, the water untouched: and the girl who gathered twigs was sad.

The Lord of Paradise heard that a man had dared to aspire to be as the Gods. Time after time he had fought the Titans, who were his peers, and kept them out of his kingdom; yet he feared a man whose power was that of suffering.

But he knew the ways of mortals, and he planned a temptation to decoy this creature of dust away from his adventure.

A breath from Paradise kissed the limbs of the girl who gathered twigs, and her youth ached with a sudden rapture of beauty, and her thoughts hummed like the bees of a rifled hive.

The time came when the ascetic should leave the forest for a mountain cave, to complete the rigour of his penance.

When he opened his eyes in order to start on this journey, the girl appeared to him like a verse familiar, yet forgotten, and which an added melody made strange. The ascetic rose from his seat and told her that it was time he left the forest.

"But why rob me of my chance to serve you?" she asked with tears in her eyes.

He sat down again, thought for long, and remained on where he was.

That night remorse kept the girl awake. She began to dread her power and hate her triumph, yet her mind tossed on the waves of turbulent delight.

In the morning she came and saluted the ascetic and asked his blessing, saying she must leave him.

He gazed on her face in silence, then said, "Go, and may your wish be fulfilled."

For years he sat alone till his penance was complete.

The Lord of the Immortals came down to tell him that he had won Paradise.

"I no longer need it," said he.

The God asked him what greater reward he desired.

"I want the girl who gathers twigs."

24

They said that Kabir, the weaver, was favoured of God, and the crowd flocked round him for medicine and miracles. But he was troubled; his low birth had hitherto endowed him with a most precious obscurity to sweeten with songs and with the presence of his God. He prayed that it might be restored.

Envious of the repute of this outcast, the priests leagued themselves with a harlot to disgrace him. Kabir came to the market to sell cloths from his loom; when the woman grasped his hand, blaming him for being faithless, and followed him to his house, saying she would not be forsaken, Kabir said to himself, "God answers prayers in his own way."

Soon the woman felt a shiver of fear and fell on her knees and cried, "Save me from my sin!" To which he said, "Open your life to God's light!"

Kabir worked at his loom and sang, and his songs washed the stains from that woman's heart, and by way of return found a home in her sweet voice.

One day the King, in a fit of caprice, sent a message to Kabir to come and sing before him. The weaver shook his head: but the messenger dared not leave his door till his master's errand was fulfilled.

The King and his courtiers started at the sight of Kabir when he entered the hall. For he was not alone, the woman followed him. Some smiled, some frowned, and the King's face darkened at the beggar's pride and shamelessness.

Kabir came back to his house disgraced, the woman fell at his feet crying, "Why accept such dishonour for my sake, master? Suffer me to go back to my infamy!"

Kabir said, "I dare not turn my God away when he comes branded with insult."

25

SOMAKA AND RITVIK

The shade of KING SOMAKA, *faring to Heaven in a chariot, passes other shades by the roadside, among them that of* RITVIK, *his former high-priest.*

A Voice: Where would you go, King?

Somaka: Whose voice is that? This turbid air is like suffocation to the eyes; I cannot see.

The Voice: Come down, King! Come down from that chariot bound for Heaven.

Somaka: Who are you?

The Voice: I am Ritvik, who in my earthly life was your preceptor and the chief priest of your house.

Somaka: Master, all the tears of the world seem to have become vapour to create this realm of vagueness. What make you here?

Shades: This hell lies hard by the road to Heaven, whence lights glimmer dimly, only to prove unapproachable. Day and night we listen to the heavenly chariot rumbling by with travellers for that region of bliss; it drives sleep from our eyes and forces them to watch in fruitless jealousy. Far below us earth's old forests rustle and her seas chant the primal hymn of creation: they sound like the wail of a memory that wanders void space in vain.

Ritvik: Come down, King!

Shades: Stop a few moments among us. The earth's tears still cling about you, like dew on freshly culled flowers. You have brought with you the mingled odours of meadow and forest; reminiscence of children, women, and comrades; something too of the ineffable music of the seasons.

Somaka: Master, why are you doomed to live in this muffled stagnant world?

Ritvik: I offered up your son in the sacrificial fire: *that* sin has lodged my soul in this obscurity.

Shades: King, tell us the story, we implore you; the recital of crime can still bring life's fire into our torpor.

Somaka: I was named Somaka, the King of Videha. After sacrificing at innumerable shrines weary year on year, a son was born to my house in my old age, love for whom, like a sudden untimely flood, swept consideration for everything else from my life. He hid me completely, as a lotus hides its stem. The neglected duties of a king piled up in shame before my throne. One day, in my audience hall, I heard my child cry from his mother's room, and instantly rushed away, vacating my throne.

Ritvik: Just then, it chanced, I entered the hall to give him my daily benediction; in blind haste he brushed me aside and enkindled my anger. When later he came back, shame-faced, I asked him: "King, what desperate alarm could draw you at the busiest hour of the day to the women's apartments, so as to desert your dignity and duty–ambassadors come from friendly courts, the aggrieved who ask for justice, your ministers waiting to discuss matters of grave import? and even lead you to slight a Brahmin's blessing?"

Somaka: At first my heart flamed with anger; the next moment I trampled it down like the raised head of a snake and meekly replied: "Having only one child, I have lost my peace of mind. Forgive me this once, and I promise that in future the father's infatuation shall never usurp the King."

Ritvik: But my heart was bitter with resentment, and I said, "If you must be delivered from the curse of having only one child, I can show you the way. But so hard is it that I feel certain you will fail to follow it." This galled the King's pride and he stood up and exclaimed, "I swear, by all that is sacred, as a Kshatriya and a King, I will not shrink, but perform whatever you may ask, however hard." "Then listen," said I. "Light a sacrificial fire, offer up your son: the smoke that rises will bring you progeny, as the clouds bring rain." The King bowed his head upon his breast and remained silent: the courtiers shouted their horror, the Brahmins clapped their hands over their ears, crying, "Sin it is both to utter and listen to such words." After some moments of bewildered dismay the King calmly said,

"I will abide by my promise." The day came, the fire was lit, the town was emptied of its people, the child was called for; but the attendants refused to obey, the soldiers rebelliously went off duty, throwing down their arms. Then I, who in my wisdom had soared far above all weakness of heart and to whom emotions were illusory, went myself to the apartment where, with their arms, women fenced the child like a flower surrounded by the menacing branches of a tree. He saw me and stretched out eager hands and struggled to come to me, for he longed to be free from the love that imprisoned him. Crying, "I am come to give you true deliverance," I snatched him by force from his fainting mother and his nurses wailing in despair. With quivering tongues the fire licked the sky and the King stood beside it, still and silent, like a tree struck dead by lightning. Fascinated by the godlike splendour of the blaze, the child babbled in glee and danced in my arms, impatient to seek an unknown nurse in the free glory of those flames.

Somaka: Stop, no more, I pray!

Shades: Ritvik, your presence is a disgrace to hell itself!

The Charioteer: This is no place for you, King! nor have you deserved to be forced to listen to this recital of a deed which makes hell shudder in pity.

Somaka: Drive off in your chariot!—Brahmin, my place is by you in this hell. The Gods may forget my sin, but can I forget the last look of agonised surprise on my child's face when, for one terrible moment, he realised that his own father had betrayed his trust?

Enter DHARMA, *the Judge of Departed Spirits*

Dharma: King, Heaven waits for you.

Somaka: No, not for me. I killed my own child.

Dharma: Your sin has been swept away in the fury of pain it caused you.

Ritvik: No, King, you must never go to Heaven alone, and thus create a second hell for me, to burn both with fire and with hatred of you! Stay here!

Somaka: I will stay.

Shades: And crown the despair and inglorious suffering of hell with the triumph of a soul!

26

The man had no useful work, only vagaries of various kinds.

Therefore it surprised him to find himself in Paradise after a life spent perfecting trifles.

Now the guide had taken him by mistake to the wrong Paradise—one meant only for good, busy souls.

In this Paradise, our man saunters along the road only to obstruct the rush of business.

He stands aside from the path and is warned that he tramples on sown seed. Pushed, he starts up: hustled, he moves on.

A very busy girl comes to fetch water from the well. Her feet run on the pavement like rapid fingers over harp-strings. Hastily she ties a negligent knot with her hair, and loose locks on her forehead pry into the dark of her eyes.

The man says to her, "Would you lend me your pitcher?"

"My pitcher?" she asks, "to draw water?"

"No, to paint patterns on."

"I have no time to waste," the girl retorts in contempt.

Now a busy soul has no chance against one who is supremely idle.

Every day she meets him at the well, and every day he repeats the same request, till at last she yields.

Our man paints the pitcher with curious colours in a mysterious maze of lines.

The girl takes it up, turns it round and asks, "What does it mean?"

"It has no meaning," he answers.

The girl carries the pitcher home. She holds it up in different lights and tries to con its mystery.

At night she leaves her bed, lights a lamp, and gazes at it from all points of view.

This is the first time she has met with something without meaning.

On the next day the man is again near the well.

The girl asks, “What do you want?”

“To do more work for you.”

“What work?” she enquires.

“Allow me to weave coloured strands into a ribbon to bind your hair.”

“Is there any need?” she asks.

“None whatever,” he allows.

The ribbon is made, and thence-forward she spends a great deal of time over her hair.

The even stretch of well-employed time in that Paradise begins to show irregular rents.

The elders are troubled; they meet in council.

The guide confesses his blunder, saying that he has brought the wrong man to the wrong place.

The wrong man is called. His turban, flaming with colour, shows plainly how great that blunder has been.

The chief of the elders says, “You must go back to the earth.”

The man heaves a sigh of relief: “I am ready.”

The girl with the ribbon round her hair chimes in: “I also!”

For the first time the chief of the elders is faced with a situation which has no sense in it.

27

It is said that in the forest, near the meeting of river and lake, certain fairies live in disguise who are only recognised as fairies after they have flown away.

A Prince went to this forest, and when he came where river met lake he saw a village girl sitting on the bank ruffling the water to make the lilies dance.

He asked her in a whisper, "Tell me, what fairy art thou?"

The girl laughed at the question and the hillsides echoed her mirth.

The Prince thought she was the laughing fairy of the waterfall.

News reached the King that the Prince had married a fairy: he sent horses and men and brought them to his house.

The Queen saw the bride and turned her face away in disgust, the Prince's sister flushed red with annoyance, and the maids asked if that was how fairies dressed.

The Prince whispered, "Hush! my fairy has come to our house in disguise."

On the day of the yearly festival the Queen said to her son, "Ask your bride not to shame us before our kinsfolk who are coming to see the fairy."

And the Prince said to his bride, "For my love's sake show thy true self to my people."

Long she sat silent, then nodded her promise while tears ran down her cheeks.

The full moon shone, the Prince, dressed in a wedding robe, entered his bride's room.

No one was there, nothing but a streak of moonlight from the window aslant the bed.

The kinsfolk crowded in with the King and the Queen, the Prince's sister stood by the door.

All asked, "Where is the fairy bride?"

The Prince answered, "She has vanished for ever to make herself known to you."

28

KARNA AND KUNTI

The Pandava Queen Kunti before marriage had a son, Karna, who, in manhood, became the commander of the Kaurava host. To hide her shame she abandoned him at birth, and a charioteer, Adhiratha, brought him up as his son.

Karna: I am Karna, the son of the charioteer, Adhiratha, and I sit here by the bank of holy Ganges to worship the setting sun. Tell me who you are.

Kunti: I am the woman who first made you acquainted with that light you are worshipping.

Karna: I do not understand: but your eyes melt my heart as the kiss of the morning sun melts the snow on a mountain-top, and your voice rouses a blind sadness within me of which the cause may well lie beyond the reach of my earliest memory. Tell me, strange woman, what mystery binds my birth to you?

Kunti: Patience, my son. I will answer when the lids of darkness come down over the prying eyes of day. In the meanwhile, know that I am Kunti.

Karna: Kunti! The mother of Arjuna?

Kunti: Yes, indeed, the mother of Arjuna, your antagonist. But do not, therefore, hate me. I still remember the day of the trial of arms in Hastina when you, an unknown boy, boldly stepped into the arena, like the first ray of dawn among the stars of night. Ah! who was that unhappy woman whose eyes kissed your bare, slim body through tears that blessed you, where she sat among the women of the royal household behind the arras? Why, the mother of Arjuna! Then the Brahmin, master of arms, stepped forth and said, "No youth of mean birth may challenge Arjuna to a trial of strength." You stood speechless, like a thunder-cloud at sunset flashing with an agony of suppressed light. But who was the woman whose heart caught fire from your shame and anger, and flared up in silence? The mother of Arjuna! Praised be Duryodhana, who perceived your worth, and then and there crowned you King of Anga, thus winning the Kauravas a champion. Overwhelmed at this good fortune, Adhiratha, the charioteer, broke through the crowd; you instantly rushed to him and laid your crown at his feet amid the jeering laughter of the Pandavas and their friends. But there was one woman of the Pandava house whose heart glowed with joy at the heroic pride of such humility;—even the mother of Arjuna!

Karna: But what brings you here alone, Mother of kings?

Kunti: I have a boon to crave.

Karna: Command me, and whatever manhood and my honour as a Kshatriya permit shall be offered at your feet.

Kunti: I have come to take you.

Karna: Where?

Kunti: To my breast thirsting for your love, my son.

Karna: Fortunate mother of five brave kings, where can you find place for me, a small chieftain of lowly descent?

Kunti: Your place is before all my other sons.

Karna: But what right have I to take it?

Kunti: Your own God-given right to your mother's love.

Karna: The gloom of evening spreads over the earth, silence rests on the water, and your voice leads me back to some primal world of infancy lost in twilit consciousness. However, whether this be dream, or fragment of forgotten reality, come near and place your right hand on my forehead. Rumour runs that I was deserted by my mother. Many a night she has come to me in my slumber, but when I cried: "Open your veil, show me your face!" her figure always vanished. Has this same dream come this evening while I wake? See, yonder the lamps are lighted in your son's tents across the river; and on this side behold the tent-domes of my Kauravas, like the suspended waves of a spell-arrested storm at sea. Before the din of tomorrow's battle, in the awful hush of this field where it must be fought, why should the voice of the mother of my opponent, Arjuna, bring me a message of forgotten motherhood? and why should my name take such music from her tongue as to draw my heart out to him and his brothers?

Kunti: 1Then delay not, my son, come with me!

Karna: Yes, I will come and never ask question, never doubt. My soul responds to your call; and the struggle for victory and fame and the rage of hatred have suddenly become untrue to me, as the delirious dream of a night in the serenity of the dawn. Tell me whither you mean to lead?

Kunti: To the other bank of the river, where those lamps burn across the ghastly pallor of the sands.

Karna: Am I there to find my lost mother for ever?

Kunti: O my son!

Karna: Then why did you banish me—a castaway uprooted from my ancestral soil, adrift in a homeless current of indignity? Why set a bottomless chasm between Arjuna and myself, turning the natural attachment of kinship to the dread attraction of hate? You remain speechless. Your shame permeates the vast darkness and sends invisible shivers through my limbs. Leave my question unanswered! Never explain to me what made you rob your son of his mother's love! Only tell me why you have come to-day to call me back to the ruins of a heaven wrecked by your own hands?

Kunti: I am dogged by a curse more deadly than your reproaches: for, though surrounded by five sons, my heart shrivels like that of a woman deprived of her children. Through the great rent that yawned for my deserted first-born, all my life's pleasures have run to waste. On that accursed day when I belied my motherhood you could not utter a word; to-day your recreant mother implores you for generous words. Let your forgiveness burn her heart like fire and consume its sin.

Karna: Mother, accept my tears!

Kunti: I did not come with the hope of winning you back to my arms, but with that of restoring your rights to you. Come and receive, as a king's son, your due among your brothers.

Karna: I am more truly the son of a charioteer, and do not covet the glory of greater parentage.

Kunti: Be that as it may, come and win back the kingdom, which is yours by right!

Karna: Must you, who once refused me a mother's love, tempt me with a kingdom? The quick bond of kindred which you severed at its root is dead, and can never grow again. Shame were mine should I hasten to call the mother of kings mother, and abandon *my* mother in the charioteer›s house!

Kunti: You are great, my son! How God's punishment invisibly grows from a tiny seed to a giant life! The helpless babe disowned by his mother comes back a man through the dark maze of events to smite his brothers!

Karna: Mother, have no fear! I know for certain that victory awaits the Pandavas. Peaceful and still though this night be, my heart is full of the music of a hopeless venture and baffled end. Ask me not to leave those who are doomed to defeat. Let the Pandavas win the throne, since they must: I remain with the desperate and forlorn. On the night of my birth you left me naked and unnamed to disgrace: leave me once again without pity to the calm expectation of defeat and death!

29

When like a flaming scimitar the hill stream has been sheathed in gloom by the evening, suddenly a flock of birds passes overhead, their loud-laughing wings hurling their flight like an arrow among stars.

It startles a passion for speed in the heart of all motionless things; the hills seem to feel in their bosom the anguish of storm-clouds, and trees long to break their rooted shackles.

For me the flight of these birds has rent a veil of stillness, and reveals an immense flutter in this deep silence.

I see these hills and forests fly across time to the unknown, and darkness thrill into fire as the stars wing by.

I feel in my own being the rush of the sea-crossing bird, cleaving a way beyond the limits of life and death, while the migrant world cries with a myriad voices, "Not here, but somewhere else, in the bosom of the Faraway."

30

The crowd listens in wonder to Kashi, the young singer, whose voice, like a sword in feats of skill, dances amidst hopeless tangles, cuts them to pieces, and exults.

Among the hearers sits old Rajah Pratap in weary endurance. For his own life had been nourished and encircled by Barajlal's songs, like a happy land which a river laces with beauty. His rainy evenings and the still hours of autumn days spoke to his heart through Barajlal's voice, and his festive nights trimmed their lamps and tinkled their bells to those songs.

When Kashi stopped for rest, Pratap smilingly winked at Barajlal and spoke to him in a whisper, "Master, now let us hear music and not this new-fangled singing, which mimics frisky kittens hunting paralysed mice."

The old singer with his spotlessly white turban made a deep bow to the assembly and took his seat. His thin fingers struck the strings of his instrument, his eyes closed, and in timid hesitation his song began. The hall was large, his voice feeble, and Pratap shouted "Bravo!" with ostentation, but whispered in his ear, "Just a little louder, friend!"

The crowd was restless; some yawned, some dozed, some complained of the heat. The air of the hall hummed with many-toned inattention, and the song, like a frail boat, tossed upon it in vain till it sank under the hubbub.

Suddenly the old man, stricken at heart, forgot a passage, and his voice groped in agony, like a blind man at a fair for his lost leader. He tried to fill the gap with any strain that came. But the gap still yawned: and the tortured notes refused to serve the need, suddenly changed their tune, and broke into a sob. The master laid his head on his instrument, and in place of his forgotten music, there broke from him the first cry of life that a child brings into the world.

Pratap touched him gently on his shoulder, and said, "Come away, our meeting is elsewhere. I know, my friend, that truth is widowed without love, and beauty dwells not with the many, nor in the moment."

31

In the youth of the world, Himalaya, you sprang from the rent breast of the earth, and hurled your burning challenges to the sun, hill after hill. Then came the mellow time when you said to yourself, "No more, no further!" and your fiery heart, that raged for the freedom of clouds, found its limits, and stood still to salute the limitless. After this check on your passion, beauty was free to play upon your breast, and trust surrounded you with thc joy of flowers and birds.

You sit in your solitude like a great reader, on whose lap lies open some ancient book with its countless pages of stone. What story is written there, I wonder?—is it the eternal wedding of the divine ascetic, Shiva, with Bhavani, the divine love?—the drama of the Terrible wooing the power of the Frail?

32

I feel that my heart will leave its own colour in all your scenes, O Earth, when I bid you farewell. Some notes of mine will be added to your seasons' melody, and my thoughts will breathe unrecognised through the cycle of shadows and sunshine.

In far-distant days summer will come to the lovers' garden, but they will not know that their flowers have borrowed an added beauty from my songs, nor that their love for this world has been deepened by mine.

33

My eyes feel the deep peace of this sky, and there stirs through me what a tree feels when it holds out its leaves like cups to be filled with sunshine.

A thought rises in my mind, like the warm breath from grass in the sun; it mingles with the gurgle of lapping water and the sigh of weary wind in village lanes,—the thought that I have lived along with the whole life of this world and have given to it my own love and sorrows.

34

I ask no reward for the songs I sang you. I shall be content if they live through the night, until Dawn, like a shepherd-maiden, calls away the stars, in alarm at the sun.

But there were moments when you sang your songs to me, and as my pride knows, my Poet, you will ever remember that I listened and lost my heart.

35

In the morning, when the dew glistened upon the grass, you came and gave a push to my swing; but, sweeping from smiles to tears, I did not know you.

Then came April's noon of gorgeous light, and I think you beckoned me to follow you.

But when I sought your face, there passed between us the procession of flowers, and men and women flinging their songs to the south wind.

Daily I passed you unheeded on the road.

But on some days full of the faint smell of oleanders, when the wind was wilful among complaining palm leaves, I would stand before you wondering if you ever had been a stranger to me.

36

The day grew dim. The early evening star faltered near the edge of a grey lonely sky.

I looked back and felt that the road lying behind me was infinitely removed; traced through my life, it had only served for a single journey and was never to be re-travelled.

The long story of my coming hither lies there dumb, in one meandering line of dust stretching from the morning hilltop to the brink of bottomless night.

I sit alone, and wonder if this road is like an instrument waiting to give up the day's lost voices in music when touched by divine fingers at nightfall.

37

Give me the supreme courage of love, this is my prayer—the courage to speak, to do, to suffer at thy will, to leave all things or be left alone.

Strengthen me on errands of danger, honour me with pain, and help me climb to that difficult mood which sacrifices daily to thee.

Give me the supreme confidence of love, this is my prayer—the confidence that belongs to life in death, to victory in defeat, to the power hidden in frailest beauty, to that dignity in pain which accepts hurt but disdains to return it.

38

TRANSLATIONS

FROM HINDI SONGS OF JNANADAS

1 Where were your songs, my bird, when you spent your nights in the nest?

Was not all your pleasure stored therein?

What makes you lose your heart to the sky—the sky that is boundless?

Answer

While I rested within bounds I was content. But when I soared into vastness I found I could sing.

2 Messenger, morning brought you, habited in gold.

After sunset your song wore a tune of ascetic grey, and then came night.

Your message was written in bright letters across black.

Why is such splendour about you to lure the heart of one who is nothing?

Answer

Great is the festival hall where you are to be the only guest.

Therefore the letter to you is written from sky to sky, and I, the proud servant, bring the invitation with all ceremony.

3 I had travelled all day and was tired, then I bowed my head towards thy kingly court still far away.

The night deepened, a longing burned in my heart; whatever the words I sang, pain cried through them, for even my songs thirsted. O my Lover, my Beloved, my best in all the world!

When time seemed lost in darkness thy hand dropped its sceptre to take up the lute and strike the uttermost chords; and my heart sang out, O my Lover, my Beloved, my best in all the world!

Ah, who is this whose arms enfold me?

Whatever I have to leave let me leave, and whatever I have to bear let me bear. Only let me walk with thee, O my Lover, my Beloved, my best in all the world!

Descend at whiles from thine audience hall, come down amid joys and sorrows; hide in all forms and delights, in love and in my heart; there sing thy songs, O my Lover, my Beloved, my best in all the world!